Bomb Proof Constructive Feedback

Sustaining Healthy Conversations at Work

Chris Zervas

ISBN:1500681989
ISBN-13: 978-1500681982

DEDICATION

To Jenna, Zoe, Elle, Kit, Nash, and Tia

CONTENTS

ACKNOWLEDGMENTS

Kristin Hanley and Neil Ward you were so helpful. You all are pros. Jenna, thank you for encouragement and proofing. Dennis Queen, Greg Conder and Nick Miller, thank you for reading and cheering. J.C., thank you for everything. Mom, thank you for modeling and teaching manners that honor.

Introduction:

In 1996, an employee of Denver's Technology Extreme Plant, was testing the quality of airbag cartridges, the explosive center of the airbag. Suddenly, a small explosion rocketed a cartridge into his sinus cavity. His sinus cavity! The man knew one wrong move -- a sneeze, a cough, a bump -- would literally blow his head off.

His colleagues understood his minimal, careful communication. So, they cautiously helped him lay down. As thoughts raced through his mind, a bomb squad member arrived and a plan initiated.

Surgeons from around the city were called. One by one, they declined. Finally a brave surgeon agreed to come to the plant and attempt to remove the cartridge – under his terms.

The surgeon requested a retaining wall with holes for his hands to be placed between him and the patient. This retaining wall would save his life if the procedure went awry.

The company agreed, and the surgery began. After forty-five frightful minutes he deftly extracted the explosive and saved the man's life.

Constructive criticism in the work place can often be just as dangerous. We say things we don't mean, recipients hear more than was meant, and minor issues detonate into major interpersonal explosions.

There is an art to giving criticism and making difficult conversations more productive for everyone.

Let's discover how we can skillfully handle difficult situations by adhering to the following principles:
1. Establish a healthy environment for difficult conversations, and
2. Deal with difficult discussions through a decision tree.

PART I. Creating a Relationally Healthy Workplace

This past fall, a friend invited me to a meeting in metropolitan Washington D.C. A group of concerned men and women gather regularly to discuss their work in changing the culture of the Carver Terrace neighborhood.

Our mid-afternoon drive looked pleasant enough. Carver Terrace seems like a nice, middle-class neighborhood. There were row houses, a beautiful view of the city, a sense of dignity, and history. Carver is named after George Washington Carver whose horticultural ingenuity saved the South's soil through crop rotation.

However, over time seeds of hatred have been sown in Carver Terrace. There are gangs, drugs, and anger among its residents.

Church's Chicken is an important marker. If you stay on the north side of the restaurant you're not 'appreciated' by those who stay on the south side of the restaurant. Violence is normal.

Following our meeting, we drove about a mile north of Carver Terrace to the National Arboretum. The arboretum "boasts nine miles of roadways that wind through glorious gardens and collections on 446 acres of trees, plants and shrubs."[i] And it is true. It is also true you can hear the gunshots at night right inside those beautiful 446 acres. The gorgeous, National Arboretum juxtaposes unhealthy Carver Terrace.

The arboretum staff meticulously care for the thousands of plants across the campus. These plants and trees flourish under the skilled leadership of the horticulturists.

Aaron is a horticulturist who works with Bonsai trees. Aaron waters, prunes and checks on his trees daily. His work is tedious. If he misses one watering, these special trees become stressed and his work intensifies. The fruits of his labor are spectacular. Aaron showed us miniature trees:

hardwoods, Maples and even a Bonsai Redwood, whose health had been restored. Thousands of tourist admire these special trees because of his dedication.

Similarly, if we are to help our company flourish, we too must embrace the sometimes tedious work to create a healthy, flourishing workplace for our personnel. A place where difficult conversations are safe, even if the workgroup across the hall is full of backstabbing and hate. Much like the arboretum to Carver Terrace, leaders have an opportunity to create a safe haven for those in our care no matter what is going on nearby.

To create an orchard of safety in our work group, we must provide the necessary components. All the trees Aaron showed me had deep chocolate-rich soil, plenty of water and plenty of sunshine, and a caregiver who helped them flourish.

The grove we want to build for our workplace is based upon those four interrelated components.

The "Service Profit Chain" -- our rich soil

Honor – life-giving water

Servant Leadership – warm, supportive sunshine.

Daily Care -- feeding and weeding

Let's go build our healthy profitable grove.

Orchard Essential I. The Rich Soil of Sincere Care

The Harvard Business Review regularly republishes articles and findings they distinguish as being significant enough to warrant repeating. These reprints are entitled, *The Best of HBR*. "Putting the Service Profit Chain to Work" originally appeared in 1994 and was reprinted in 2008. In it, author James Heskett and his colleagues explain research revealing a distinct link between "internal service quality" and "profitability." This work was later expanded upon in the book, The Service Profit Chain.

Their chain is based on these components:

Internal Service Quality
Employee Satisfaction
Employee Loyalty
Employee Productivity
External Service Value
Customer Satisfaction

Customer Loyalty
Profitability[ii]

The authors state:

∞ Profitability is based on customer loyalty.
∞ Customer loyalty is built on customer satisfaction.
∞ Satisfaction is driven by the belief customers are receiving an "external service value."
∞ External Service value stems from employees who are productive.
∞ Loyal employees are more productive.
∞ Satisfied employees are loyal.
∞ Employee satisfaction grows from an internal service quality

Internal Service Quality

The anchor link of the service profit chain is internal service quality. It is defined by the authors as:

"Company leaders who actively develop and maintain a company culture centered around sincere care and service to fellow employees and customers"
(emphasis mine). [iii]

The findings of Heskett and his team are confirmed in similar research

4

by Ken Blanchard[iv] and the principle is stated simply by Oriental Trading Post CEO, Sam Taylor:

"Number 1, we'll take care of our employees. Number 2, we'll let our employees take care of our customers. Number 3, we'll let our customers take care of spreading the word – and then everything else will take care of itself."

Brand inside must equal your brand outside.

The authors frequently mention Southwest Airlines in the original Harvard Business Review article. Southwest Airlines co-founder, Herb Kelleher, was a man of superior vision. In the seventies, Kelleher began Southwest airlines with what was called "The Love Triangle". His three-plane fleet flew from Dallas's Love field to San Antonio to Houston and back to Dallas.

Kelleher's leadership morphed his Texas triangle into the most successful airline in the United States. They now have over 3,100 flights per day. A former Southwest pilot shared that when Kelleher entered a room, his personality filled it. After 37 years at Southwest, he was asked about the secrets to his success. His entire response? "You have to treat your employees like customers."[v]

> "You have to treat your employees like customers."
>
> Herb Kelleher, founder Southwest Airlines

On his retirement, the SWA pilots union took out a full-page ad in USA Today thanking him for all he had done. Ironically, across town in Dallas, American Airlines' pilots were picketing the Annual Meeting. Kelleher's personnel, on the other hand, were satisfied and grateful. They felt respected and cared for by the company.

Sincere care for which feeds everyone – a soil of sincere care and team members is demonstrated not solely in communication celebrating victories, but also correcting detrimental behavior. People appreciate honest correction more than flattery, wrote Solomon thousands of years ago.[vi] It is up to us to learn to communicate this correction in a manner that builds up our team. Our work groups flourish in this type of soil --rich, deep, dark, nutritious soil service to employees.

Orchard Essential II. The Life Giving Water of Honor

Honor simply means we value others. Honor is defined by Merriam-Webster as "a showing of usually merited respect"[vii]

Honor is a concept that author and speaker Gary Smalley constructed his entire career upon. Smalley's resources on relationships have sold in the millions. He has wisely capitalized on the concept of honor, for it is a value we all long to receive.

In addition, honor has been a component of cultures in the Middle East since ancient times. Moses was given the Ten Commandments. Of the ten, one was the command to honor your father and mother.

Honor's presence in a relationship brings nourishment, for it escorts respect alongside. With respect comes humility, and typically, interpersonal peace. Honor is the life-giving water to all relationships. It sustains and fuels a relationship.

Thousands of years after the Ten Commandments, another leader exemplified this concept well. In our Civil War, General Ulysses S. Grant carried himself as a leader who honored both his soldiers and his enemies. This honor is described in a confederate soldier's diary:

"The [Union senior] officers rode past the

Confederates smugly without any sign of recognition
except by one. 'When General Grant reached the line
of ragged, filthy, bloody, despairing prisoners strung
out on each side of the bridge, he lifted his hat and
held it over his head until he passed the last man of
that living funeral cortege. He was the only officer in
that whole train who recognized us as being on the
face of the earth."[viii]

"We are Ladies and Gentlemen Serving Ladies and Gentlemen." Hotelier Horst Schulze, grasped the importance of honoring in his leadership of the growth of Ritz-Carlton hotels. Schulze coined the company's well-known customer-centered credo. Though the concept of honor is often overlooked in our Western hurry-up goal oriented workplace, Schulze realizes its need.

Demonstrating esteem and value for your fellow workers sets the groundwork for communicating difficult messages. It allows us to successfully deliver our carefully planned messages without them blowing up in our face.

Orchard Essential III. The Sunshine of Servant Leadership

The World's Most Powerful Leadership Principle: How to Become a Servant Leader by James Hunter is an outstanding read on leading our teams as a servant and doing so with integrity.

The term, "Servant Leadership," was first coined by AT&T executive Robert Greenleaf in the 1960's. Greenleaf reasoned that a better society (or workplace) would be one in which leaders served under the direction of a moral compass and sought to serve their employees so the employees could better accomplish their job.

To further understand the concept, consider John F. Kennedy's famous words paraphrased for a servant leader:

Ask not what your employees can do for you, but
what you can do for your employees.

A servant leader doesn't expect for others to meet his needs, but looks at individuals in his organization and determines how he can meet their needs for their good, and ultimately for the good of the organization. It's not just about one person taking advantage of another, but about two people learning how to help one another and work toward a common goal for the good of everyone (including the overarching business) as a whole.

Servant leadership is the sunshine providing photosynthesis for growth. As Hunter describes, it is indeed the world's most powerful leadership principle. The act of serving, itself, being the core of the energy. It's steady, positive influence provides security for long term growth – a future return for those you are serving and for the company.

The agenda that servant leaders set is for the good of the organization itself, but most importantly, for the improvement of the people within that organization.[ix] The servant leader leads in order to better serve others, not increase his or her own power. In doing so, both parties ultimately benefit from the leader taking this role and producing fruit feeding the company.

With this as a backdrop, you can be free to discuss difficult concepts with your workers, because people can sense motivation. If you are truly set on their well-being, they'll relax and embrace your words. Hunter contrasts authority and influence.

Authority is defined as "the ability to force or coerce someone to do your will, even if they would choose not to, because of your position or might."[x]

Authority flashes quick results of apparent success, but there is no telling what the long-term damage will be. Think of a ranting boss who gets his way because of his yelling and screaming. You've had them, and we all know you just go on because . . . well, they are your boss.

The Queen Mary II was docked in California. For years the ship had been a tourist site. She had been faithfully painted and kept clean. There was a push to have her revitalized to be seaworthy again. As the refurbishment project began, the smoke stacks were studied. Surprisingly, they found there was no steel left in them at all. They were simply being held up by years of white paint application.

Like the ship's smoke stacks, an authoritarian approach is a quick fix. It has no depth or true strength and is held up by position only.

On the other hand, Hunter defines influence as the skill of getting people to willingly do your will because of your personal influence[xi] – this is the essence of Servant Leadership.

Influence doesn't often display immediate results – it is an investment. However, it leaves long-term healthy fruit.

Ponder the influences in your life. You are who you are because of influencers. A loving influence is powerful. You understand they truly have an interest in you and your well-being.

Jesse Owens is considered one of the greatest track athletes of all time. Owens grew up the youngest of 10 children to a poor, sharecropping family in the south. Sickness plagued him as a child and almost died due to breathing problems.

Even so, Charles Riley, a track coach at Cleveland's Fairmont Junior High school noticed the speed of young Jesse Owens. From there Owen's accomplishments are legendary.

In the spring of 1935, Owens fell down stairs while horsing around with friends. He wasn't sure he would be able to race at the Big 10 Championships in Ann Arbor, Michigan. The first race was the 100-yard dash.

Stiffly, Owens settled into the blocks and from the firing of the starter's pistol, the Buckeye Bullet never looked back. Within 45 minutes he had tied or equaled four WORLD records. Those wins on one day have been chosen as the most impressive athletic day since 1850.[xii]

Owens, a black American, went on to win four gold medals at the 1936 Olympic Games in Berlin, just as Hitler was touting the supremacy of the Arian Race. Yet, when he was asked to what he attributed his success, he testified to the encouragement of his original coach, Charles Riley.

Riley served Owens by encouraging him and meeting his physical needs when he was unable to provide for himself. Owens would have breakfast at Riley's home when things were tight in his home. Riley would provide shoes to Owens as a boy when the Owen's family couldn't afford them.

Charles Riley's influence and servant hood impacted the world through Jesse Owens' track career.

At times leaders do need to reload power into their authority cache. When personnel don't do as you ask, they get discipline, etc. If they

> *The key to successful leadership today is influence, not authority.*
> **Kenneth Blanchard**

continually do not modify their behavior, they are fired. Watch one episode of Donald Trump in "The Apprentice." There you'll see the exercise of raw authority.

However, many famous world leaders have sacrificed their authority and led by great influence undergirded with integrity. Mother Teresa, Mahatma Gandhi, Jesus the Messiah, Abraham Lincoln and General George Marshall exemplify servant leadership styles which empowered and mobilized their followers. Those they led were able to conquer and achieve more through edification and support than through coercion or manipulation.

Mother Teresa laid down her life for the infirmed of India. She chose to sacrifice her comfort for the needs of people no one else would love. Today, her Sisters of Charity care for sick around the world.

Gandhi laid down his life for the nation of India to be free from British rule. Through his servant leadership, he led a seemingly powerless British colony to bring a world power to its knees. The long-term fruit of his work? India is poised to become one of the leading economic powers on the planet.

Jesus' words capture the essence a servant leader, "There is no greater love than to lay down one's life for one's friends."[xiii] He laid down his life for his friends to forgive them of their moral imperfections. His fruit is innumerable and his followers number more than anyone in history.

Abraham Lincoln's lasting impact on the United States is daily assumed by most as normalcy. Yet without his courage the preservation of the Union and the freeing of slaves would be missing.

"Lincoln's aspiration to become President stemmed from his desire to serve his country. This suggests that Lincoln did not seek the position of executive leader solely for the sake of power that such an opportunity would create for him. He understood that the Presidency was the ultimate position to serve his fellow Americans and move the country toward a 'more perfect Union.' The position of executive leader would provide him with the platform necessary to fulfill this vision for the people and the nation."[xiv]

Abraham Lincoln was a statesman. A statesman. He envisioned the greater good and sought the position to accomplish it.

Another American, forward-thinking General George Marshall staked the rebuilding of today's leading countries. It has been said that while others were thinking of war, Marshall was thinking of peace; when others were thinking of peace, Marshall was thinking of war. He is the author of "The Marshall Plan" which helped rebuild Europe following WWII.

Marshall inspired others through his servant leadership. He picked many American generals who were leaders in WWII, including Lloyd Fredendall, Leslie McNair, Mark Wayne Clark and Omar Bradley.

In all it is estimated he trained 200 officers who became generals in WWII.[xv] One pupil in particular caught his attention. He recognized young Dwight had the potential to be a better leader than himself, so Marshall poured himself into Dwight and equipped him with all he knew. Marshall understood Dwight Eisenhower could be a great leader of our country, and he promoted and poured himself into Eisenhower's success.

George Marshall laid down his ambitions for Dwight Eisenhower. Abraham Lincoln laid down his life for slaves and his country. Jesus laid down his life for his followers. Gandhi laid down his life for his country. Mother Teresa laid down her life for the sick. And because of their servant leadership, they are respected and followed long after their deaths.

These examples of Servant Leaders show us how to serve our personnel for the better of our organization. Let me offer hope to you; you can begin to change your thought process to serve those who expect you want them to serve you.

Orchard Essential IV. Weeding and Feeding is Correction and Praise

The last essential principle of our grove requires us to be proactive growers. As we continue the plant analogy, we must supply the daily care to create and maintain an environment for plants (our employees) to flourish.

Today's one application feed and seed fertilizer portrays an easy fix for horticultural problems. Yet, a chemical approach to providing food for our personnel and protecting them from weeds, thorns and insects is not so simple.

Providing feedback both positive and negative to those we lead is consistent, hard work. We must be present, attentive, and courageous. An absent leader cannot be attentive. Leadership also necessitates courage to confront poor performance and celebrate victories.

As we just discussed, Servant Leadership proclaims feedback we give should be based on helping the employee grow.

Typically, four reasons exist for feedback given to employees

- To meet required assessment schedules
- To satisfy the leader's desires
- To improve an employee's competence
- To improve an employee's commitment[xvi]

The bottom two reasons for feedback are the most valid if we are to grow a healthy orchard. To show why, let's first assess reasons one and two.

One reason to give feedback is that it is required. For example, according to company policy, we must provide a six-month performance review. Feedback from requirement shouts of duty, and can echo a lack of interest in a worker.

As a young retail worker, I was given an annual review. It began with words delivered obligatorily. "All right, we have to do this review." My boss had to document a completion of evaluations. The event was shorter than a commercial break and featured phrases such as, "You are doing fine," and "work on this."

I was a young man, striving to make a difference in my world. I left the discussion feeling completely irrelevant. I also felt cheated out of information that could help me grow in my position to impact the work culture.

Another reason we give feedback is to satisfy our own needs. If this feedback is based on our own insecurity, it can be equally as destructive for the good of the company and the employee. Self-centered motivation is not based on a team member's future, the company's success, but on our own ego or survival. This type of feedback is very prevalent but is often fueled by wrong motives – most often myopic.

Most all of us have been guilty of giving feedback to others for our benefit alone. We often want to control the environment. We must be careful in our efforts to make sure we are thinking not of ourselves, but others and our company. Ultimately, if we elevate the needs of the company and value personnel, we have sought the greater good.

The last two reasons for feedback provide light and life to our team and organization.

The third reason to give feedback is to improve proficiency. Think of your hobbies. Are you a golfer? A good golf coach can take several strokes off your score. Yet, if we continue in our bad habits, we don't improve and continue to make the same mistakes. The same goes for a good leader who gives timely feedback; they make a difference in those we pay for performance.

> *"The opportunity loss is tremendous," explains Susan Fowler, a senior consulting partner with The Ken Blanchard Companies. "We know from the research that if someone does not get feedback, they are not going to grow. If they get feedback that is ill-delivered or ill-defined, then their performance can even decline. The only way we see a dependable increase in performance is when a person gets well-crafted, targeted feedback in a timely fashion."*[xvii]

Lastly, great feedback can improve commitment. With proper coaching, players improve. With improvement often comes greater commitment and dedication. As we learned in the first orchard essential, "The Service Profit Chain," satisfied employees are loyal employees. Employee satisfaction stems from employees who feel sincere care from their leaders. Timely, effective feedback is part of care.

With a focus on their success, instead of ourselves, we can help our personnel grow above their expectations. Director Robert Altman said it this way in his Oscar acceptance speech:

"The role of the Director is to create a space where
the actors and actresses can become more than
they've ever been before, more than they've
dreamed of being."

We are directors. Day in and day out. Our focus should be on creating soil where our flowers flourish and become more than they ever dreamed of being.

Let's now move toward discussing how we energize our workplace for a dream-giving setting.

Feeding the Plants

"As we express our gratitude, we must never forget that the highest appreciation is not to utter words, but to live by them."

— President **John F. Kennedy**

One daily, critical task is feeding the soil. When the soil is rich, the plants are free to flourish and enjoy all the accoutrements of a well-tended garden.

For our workplace fertilization, we turn to legendary business leader, Ken Blanchard. Blanchard and Robert Johnson authored a timeless leadership book, *The One Minute Manager*. The authors share that leading people moment-by-moment is critical for leaders, those they lead, and the company as a whole.

One minute managing is divided into two components. The first is one-minute praising. The second is one-minute correction. Let's sing about one-minute praising first.

Todd Vinson, founder of Willow Springs Boy's Ranch provides stable homes to troubled boys and helps them grow from boys to men. One famous quote he often shares with his staff is: "Catch 'em doing right."

When our eyes catch our staff members doing right, we should let them know.

The One-Minute Manager encourages this sequence after "Catching 'em doing right."

- Praise people immediately
- Tell people what they did right – be specific
- Tell people how good you feel about what they did right, how it helps the organization and their co-workers
- Stop for a moment of silence to let them "feel" how good you feel
- Shake hands, or pat on the back, etc. – in a way that tells them you support their success in the organization[xviii]

This simple process is fertilizer for the roots of our teams. Brian Brandt was the former CEO of Sky Ranch Camp. While there, he had a maintenance man go way out of his way to address plumbing problems. Under buildings, through grime and more, the gentleman crawled to accomplish the task. It was a supreme effort and one beyond the call of duty.

To thank him, Brian called him at home in the evening. The conversation went something like this:

Brian: "Hey Melvin, I was calling to say thanks for the plumbing job you did today. I really appreciate all your effort."
Melvin: "Oh, you are welcome."
Brian: "Well, it was a great job; so thank you for your hard work."
Melvin: "Oh, it wasn't a big deal. So why'd you call?"
Brian: "Well, I just called to say thanks for your work today."
Melvin: "Great, so why'd you call?"
Brian: "No really, I just called to say thank you. You worked hard today and did what no one else could do, so thank you."

This staffer finally grasped the message; he was being thanked with no agenda and no ulterior message motive. As you can imagine, he was soon able to tell his wife and others at home who asked, "Who was on the phone? What did they want?" Brian bolstered the attitude of one of his men who would now go through a wall for him.

Catching people doing right energizes the company. Encouragement fuels staffers to go beyond the call of duty to greater effort.

Geese provide a great example of encouragement's power.

Geese fly 71% farther as a team in a "V" formation than they can by themselves. As they fly behind each other, one bird takes the brunt of the force of the wind by being the point of the "V". As it flaps its wings, the birds behind are beneficiaries of lift created by the force of the wings. When they fly out of formation, they soon realize it.

Additionally, if a goose is injured, at least two other geese will fly down with it and join it until the bird is well enough to fly. When flight is re-started, again a "V" formation is used to join the flock.

Part of their teamwork's success is accelerated through encouragement. Researchers have discovered geese are "honking" encouragement. Their honking is not a complaint, rather a cheer to "keep going, don't stop. We are going to get to the beach tonight!" Together.

My father was a fantastic storyteller. One of my favorite jokes he delivered was about geese flying in formation. He'd ask, "Have you ever seen geese fly in formation, like a "V?" His audience would always acquiesce. He'd then ask them if they had ever noticed one side was longer than the other on the "V" and how they never were exactly equal. And, of course, the audience would say "Yes, we have noticed." He'd then ask if they knew why that was; why one side of the "V" was longer than the other. When they answered, "no", he'd reply that the long side had more geese on it!

Like geese, we should encourage our colleagues with words which share in their victories. We have an opportunity to create "lift" for our fellow workers.

We should encourage often; not waiting until a job is complete. At football games, fans do not sit mute as the ball moves down the field, waiting for a touchdown before cheering. No, fans erupt for first downs, strong runs, and great catches. We should do the same in our workplace as progress is made. Encouragement is extremely powerful to the morale of individuals and a team.

How Full is Your Bucket? expounds upon the findings of Gallup Polls regarding encouragement. Gallup surveyed more than 4 million employees worldwide. The surveys were across 30 industries and over 10,000 business units. They found employees who had received regular praise and encouragement had:

- increased their individual productivity
- increased engagement among their colleagues
- were more likely to stay with their organization
- received higher loyalty and satisfaction scores from customers
- had better safety records and fewer accidents on the job[xix]

To put the balance in perspective let's gaze at the two primary components of the workplace. The workplace has two tracks like a train. One track consists of processes, goals, tasks, measurements, and finances which make a business profitable. People and relationships comprise the other. A bent, broken or missing rail stops the train.

For example, if all our focus at work were upon relationships/encouragement and we had no requirements such as goals, deadlines, projects and accountability, we would ultimately have a bankrupt business with a stable full of resentful staffers. Our discouraged employees would have learned and achieved nothing while employed/led by us.

Relationship

<u>- Requirements</u>

Resentment[xx]

Yet on the opposite end of the spectrum is a company where work is King and employees are pawns. There is little relational encouragement from the leader and requirements, deadlines, production and end results are the only focus. This type of leader just wants the work done-- nothing else. The staff can grow so frustrated with requirements and a lack of personal connection, tyranny can soon arise.

Requirements

<u>- Relationship</u>

Rebellion[xxi]

I once worked in an organization with two distinct branches. One was operational. The other was financial.

Our fledgling organization's staff could gather around one small table for lunch. The senior member on the operating side was the day-to-day leader. I was on the financial side and, ultimately, reported to the President of the Board.

He clearly communicated to me I was not part of his operating team. He often stressed my exclusion. His stance created division within the organization; it climaxed personally one day when he appeared in my office suddenly with a question. He asked, "Do you think of me as your boss?"

"No, not really," I answered.

"Good," he replied, exiting my space.

The implication from his other actions was that he didn't want a relationship. He didn't want to deal with the responsibility of our side of the business and with a relationship with me. He did, however, want us to fulfill our responsibilities financially.

Did I grow in my respect of him? Absolutely not. His insecurity led to division within the organization plaguing it for many years. Leadership such as this creates rebellion.

However, a leader who balances the work and relational needs of workers helps create a prosperous, interdependent, unified environment. People are given tasks and are held responsible to deliver professional results professionally on time. Care presents itself equally strong through connection with workers as human beings. If this type of balance is reached, you have created an environment of respect.

Requirements

+ <u>Relationship</u>

Respect[xxii]

I once worked for a very strong leader, who also exhibited great care for his staff. He did a great job of listening to my professional and personal needs. Yet, he was not shy about getting in my face.

One day, he did. I had made decisions he didn't appreciate and he let me know about it. I, dejected, ambled to my friend, who also worked for him, and shared my misery.

At the next meeting with my boss, he asked if I had shared negatively about our discussion with my friend. "Yes Sir", I stated. He then passionately explained how I was destroying morale, and if I had a problem with him, to speak to him first.

I was wrong.

My strong leader was right.

I deserved the tongue lashing I received.

He earned the respect I still have.

Can we Over Fertilize?

Soil acidity is a delicate balance. If a soil is too acidic, it can burn up the roots of a plant. If the soil is too alkaline, most plants fail to thrive.

Researchers Barbara Fredrickson and Marcial Losada are mathematicians who have found interesting research on the power of praise. Just as healthy soil required chemical balance, mathematical research confirms a balance must exist between praise and correction.

3:1   VS.   13:1

Fredrickson and Losada[xxiii][xxiv] discovered praising must fall within a

19

certain volume in relationship to other interactions. Life at work is not all "Blue Sky".

If our interactions of positive to negative conversations are less than three to one, relationships suffer.

For example, think of someone in your life who offers more correction than praise; this person doesn't balance praise with his criticism Do you want to be around them? No, you always fear they will "bomb" you with every other sentence.

On the other hand think of someone who always tells you how wonderful you are and never has any correction? You begin to realize this person has no balance, and they don't have the courage to tell the truth; they seem more interested in flattering you. This is the case when positive to negative comments are greater than 13:1 according to Fredrickson and Losada.

Now think about people who truly care for you. You know they will encourage you when you need it; they will also get in your face if need be. Leaders such as this are ones you want to follow.

As in everything, balance is key. Hopefully, your organizations has hired the right people and it is simple to have your praises far outnumber your corrections.

Weeding your Soil

Corn grown without synthetic fertilizer that is "knee-high by the fourth of July" is a fruit of hard labor. This type of corn is probably knee-high to a calloused knee.

Great farmers perpetually weed around their crops. If they don't weed regularly, they will have dragon-sized weeds stealing life out of the soil. Soil provides only so much nutrition.

Similarly, in the workplace we either spend our energies fighting fires and problems or expend it toward creativity, progress and success.

Weeding the orchard or your workplace regularly generates the power and life-giving freedom of the one-minute manager. Weeding is addressing detrimental behavior. Weeding is a natural part of the harvesting process. It must be done.

Correction on an as-needed basis aids staff development. Still, many people hate correcting those they lead. Authors Greef and De Bruyne studied five ways people typically respond to their need to correct:

- Accommodation/smoothing
- Avoidance/withdrawal
- Compromise
- Competition/forcing

- Collaboration/problem-solving[xxv]

Most of us have been guilty of the first four responses to conflict. We do what we can to keep peace, when sharpening of others is what is needed. Yet, in the workplace, we are often called to sharpen another employee. When we do, sparks can fly.

The sparks are producing results. The instrument being sharpened is undergoing pain, but ultimately, the pain will produce a more useful tool.

When we don't sharpen our personnel, we are not honoring them or others in our organization. When we accommodate and smooth a staffer who is misbehaving, we don't honor others on our team.

When we avoid or withdraw from a worker whose conduct needs reprimanding, we are not honoring him/her. Our responsibility is to lead and provide growth and nurture to the worker for the good of our organization.

When we compromise the rules for one staffer who isn't following them, we are not honoring others who are forced to keep the guidelines of the organization. Additionally, we are not honoring the founders or leaders who established the rules.

And the last common, unhealthy conflict response problem involves forcing an employee to obey. When we force behavior, we are not honoring the individual; it is an exhibition of raw positional authority not the beauty of influence.

However, when we collaborate and problem-solve we honor them and all others in the organization. It takes courage, effort and good listening skills, but collaborating supplies our workers with confidence to know you are a leader who will care for them.

In summary, our guide for daily leadership is *The One-Minute Manager*. The other message of the classic book from Blanchard and Johnson is the moment by moment leadership of correction. Every day we must stop detrimental behavior in which our staffers are engaged. We have an eye out for areas needing improvement.

The book describes two halves of the correction. In summary, there are three points to address in the first half of the correction and three in the second half.

1. *Correct people as soon as possible.*

When we don't enact justice quickly, weed roots grow deeper. Workers may begin to reason they can get away with a certain behavior, and, therefore, it becomes more common. As well, the others in a department can begin to have more and more negative thoughts about fairness.

2. *Almost always correct privately.*

No one likes their dirty laundry aired out on Main Street. Let your worker understand what behavior needs correction – not anyone else.

The exception to this rule would be to a fellow leader who has reverted back in policy to an outdated, detrimental procedure. These types of things can be done in public to reaffirm the course of the company's future.

3. Be specific in your correction.

When we are not specific, the staffer may unknowingly repeat the offense. It is up to us to clearly define the wrong, and if necessary, share why it is detrimental to the team.

Wise farmers know if they have an unhealthy plant, cautious weeding is best. If they have not invested in the front end of creating a safe, healthy, nutritious garden, the weeding must be done extra carefully to not damage the plant in the process. The same is true of our workplace. We should focus on workplace stability before embarking on correction.

Healing After Weeding

After getting to the meat of the issue with a team member, we need to rebuild the relationship. As we learned from researchers Fredrickson and Losada there must be a majority of interactions focused on encouragement. Blanchard and Johnson stress the importance here. The second-half of the correction process re-balances the tension of the task (the reason for the reprimand) and relationship – which is now our focus.

- Shake hands, pat on the back, etc…, in a way that lets them know you are honestly on their side.
- Reaffirm you think well of them and their service to the organization. Your words help those you are leading understand they are in good graces with you and the entire team.
- Realize when the reprimand is over, it is over completely. [xxvi]

What's in it for You?

Helping your staff and helping your company has been our focus. And true, there are benefits for you indirectly – if you are a leader, your company can be much more prosperous as we learned through the Service Profit Chain.

But what about you as a person? Work is stressful. Having employees can be difficult, and your leadership of them consumes much of your waking, even your sleeping, thoughts.

However, actively leading your staff, creating a healthy orchard, and dealing with issues that call for attention may have its greatest impact on you, your health and your joy.

When I work with companies on this topic, I illustrate my point by donning a backpack full of bricks and flowers. Then I share the following:

It is important to note that leading as a one-minute manager is critical for our wellbeing, the wellbeing of the staff, and the wellbeing of the organization. Many of us bring our difficult workers home with us. Our spouses know about them. We carry them around with us like bricks in a backpack. Every time we don't deal with a worker's detrimental behavior which bothers us, we are adding a brick in our backpack.

We may carry difficult staffers around so much our children know about them. We may interact with our children in a way influenced by the stress of that person.

In fact, we may carry these heavy bricks around so much that even our doctor knows about them.

When we manage moment by moment, as the one-minute manager teaches us, we are keeping bricks from piling up in our backpack. When we discuss with our team members how their actions are difficult for the team, we are instead emptying our backpack daily.

In fact, true correction is not only taking bricks out of our backpack, but it is really giving a gift to our staffers. We are giving them a blessing, a flower, to teach them how they are to act and respond.

Again, "True correction is appreciated more than flattery".[xxvii]

PART II: When Difficult, Deeper Conversations are Necessary

Despite the fact we have watered, fed, weeded and cared for our plants, at times our plants need help to grow straight. They may be struggling with dead limbs, areas eaten by insects and animals, or branches withered or growing incorrectly.

These impurities restrict our crop from producing fruit, can interfere with other crop growth, and can expose the rest of the crop to danger or infection.

Wise farmers consistently prune these areas on their plants. Pruning involves cutting away small pieces of unhealthy growth. Great growers understand when, where and how to prune a plant for its more full-term health. They know leaving plants to themselves will ultimately lead to areas of neglect and dysfunction.

If a plant has been fed well, has plenty of water, sunshine, and daily care, pruning is a source of life. The short-term pain strengthens roots, stabilizes the plant and stimulates production of more fruit.

Similarly, our workers need pruning. By pruning, I am talking about dealing with behavior needing confrontation. These areas may be bad habits, poor choices, or emotional injury which plays itself out in unhealthy ways.

In Part I, we addressed how to manage small events occurring day-to-day. In Part II, we'll focus on a decision tree to guide us through communication to solve more serious happenings or events which have been brewing and need attention.

It is important to revisit authority and influence as Blanchard describes. If we have managed with manipulative authority, have not encouraged, and our staff feels their value is based on performance, we have not provided a good root system for the trees.

Just as pruning may cripple an already unhealthy plant, condemnation may do the same. Condemnation is a powerful motivator – for the short term. But without stability, condemnation will ultimately hurt the person, the team, and the company.

If, on the other hand, we are influential leaders who have displayed servant leadership, service, and plenty of encouragement, our corrections will not be threatening, but empowering for workers to move forward with freedom.

A grower's goal is a healthy crop producing stability, shade and fruit for others. This translates to a valuable employee who gets work done, assists others and is a stable, healthy contributor.

Difficult discussions require several keys to get the results we seek. To produce a fruitful office, we should use the following decision tree:

1. Take a personal inventory
2. Be "I"nterrogative
3. Confront Honorably
4. Look to the Future

Decision Branch I. Take A Personal Inventory

We must first peek under our own hood. We've got to understand our motivation before we can move forward.

All of us are hard-wired with a God-given inclination regarding conflict. We either run or gun. Runners prefer to avoid confrontation. Gunners set their sights on conflict as a challenge; they are ready to shoot it out to the end.

So part of our personal inventory is asking ourselves a few questions. If we are runners we should ask: "Is this an issue I need to deal with, but have chosen to avoid?"

For gunners, the question is quite different: "Is this an issue I am making a big deal out of because I want to fight?"

First-century leader James, wrote

"We should be quick to listen, slow to speak and slow to become angry."[xxviii]

He goes on to share that our selfish desires cause fights and quarrels among us.[xxix]

Look At Yourself First

Introspection may expose the real issue to be one residing in our own heart. It may not be our co-worker's fault at all; we may be struggling with an issue internally with which we need to deal.

Our selfish desires can be difficult to see.

I once misplaced my temper with a staffer who was simply resting. I was leading a small team operating a five-room guest hotel at a sports camp for urban children. Daily, we hosted new guests who were donors to the non-profit. Our work was to be an entire hotel staff to our guests. We wore the hats of housekeepers, concierges, bellmen, waiters, receptionists and maintenance engineers. As one of my first forays into leadership, I was

28

wound up tighter than a ten-day clock, for all the wrong reasons.

I rarely rested and worked 16 hour days, simply out of anxiety. My expectation was for all those working with me to keep the same pace. One morning after doing what was mandatory service work for our guest, I found an employee resting on his bed. I didn't look fondly upon it.

In his defense, he simply didn't know what he needed to be doing. I had failed to share what position he needed to fill next. Underlying my frustration was a very selfish desire to impress my leaders. I was driven to seek the approval of my superiors, not lead my team. My unhealthy work, work, work ethic was the real problem.

My outburst hurt my relationship with the employee, relationships with others and ultimately weakened our team.

So, as leaders, we must gaze at the man or woman in the mirror and ask, "Is this my issue? Or is it truly an issue this person needs direction in?"

Susan Fowler says it this way,

"I think that oftentimes, sadly, the feedback that we do give to people is based on our own need to be seen as an expert or to control the environment." To address this, Fowler recommends that managers ask themselves, "Is this my need to give this feedback or am I giving this feedback because the other person's performance will actually benefit as a result of it?"[xxx]

A little introspection is vital before we go "helping someone else".

Try To Understand Your Co-Worker

Copernicus, who lived from 1473-1543, received a royal burial at a Polish mass in 2010. Copernicus was a genius. He asserted the earth revolved around the sun; that the sun was the center of the universe. At the time Copernicus was viewed heretically, for his views opposed those of the church. Yet, his discovery impacts us all.

Like the people of Copernicus' day, we are often blinded in our approach to a central, human-nature, truth. We tend to act as though the world revolves around us.

Therefore, the next step in our personal inventory is to try and understand the offender. They too think the world revolves around them. If the issue is not about us, what motivates the actions of the worker? What do they value most? Fear most? Is his home life a mess? Is he out to get someone? Was it just an oversight? Does he just think differently? All of these questions must be answered before moving forward, and may deliver us from future conflicts as well.

If the answer to these questions sheds light on the situation, we must respond accordingly. For example, perhaps the team member is experiencing a divorce. Research suggests divorce can impact an employee's productivity for up to three years.[xxxi]

By proceeding with an others-centered lens you can begin a gradual change of your culture; one focusing on others, the team and the big picture.

Forgive Your Co-Worker

What is the next step in our personal inventory? Make a choice to forgive. We must live as Nelson Mandela. Mandela, who, after 30 years of imprisonment at the hands of the Afrikaners, was finally released and then elected president of his country. Instead of imposing laws to retaliate against oppressors, he chose instead to love, and lead a life of forgiveness for the well-being of his organization, the nation of South Africa.

If you do not forgive them? You will be the one who suffers. You can forgive them now, or pay for it later.

Forgiveness is a choice to exhibit charity toward another person. It is a choice to release them from owing you anything. The Gift of Forgiveness by Charles Stanley is an outstanding read on this sometimes difficult choice.

Forgiveness isn't easy, but it is a decision of our will, not a feeling. The feelings may come and go, but forgiveness says you value the person regardless of performance.

The last choice in the personal inventory is waiting.

Wait Until Your Anger Has Subsided

Self-control and logic are not by-products of anger. We may have stepped systematically through the above steps in a personal inventory, but if our tachometer and our face show a red background, wait.

We must allow our face to retain its color and bring our internal motor back to idle speed. It is important that we allow ourselves to calm down before we talk about an issue with a team member. Quick-rising anger can be destructive. Conversely, contemplative, understanding and properly-placed anger can be extremely effective.

For example, think of how many emails you have sent out in haste and then wished you could get them back. Think, as well, of the many words you have said in haste and then later wanted them back. Effective feedback is delivered from a still heart, not one raging with anger. As you know, you can catch more bees with honey than vinegar.

Decision Branch II. Be "I"nterrogative

Wise men from century to century continue to tell us that we need to listen before we speak. Yet, we have all made the mistake of confronting before hearing the whole story.

A difficult conversation is not a lecture; it is a discussion. We arrive equipped with two ears and one mouth. Exercising this ratio, at this time, is vital. Before we foolishly unload a double-barrel-cannon shot, we need to first discover their side of the story.

These discussions supply a fantastic opportunity for you to build sincere care into your workplace through world-class listening. You should turn off phones, eliminate distractions and focus your full attention.

This ancient Asian symbol for listening illuminates listening as more than a one-organ performance. Listening should incorporate our eyes, ears and heart. Our eyes should be centered on them, our ears attentive only to them and our heart involved in their side of the story.

Listening to their response to open-ended questions is one of the best techniques we can employ.

To lead the conversation, begin with blame-free, unemotional questions about the situation. The questions most often contain the word "I". We are not accusing or prosecuting them (using the word "you"); we are gathering information for ourselves. For example:

"I was leaving work last night and noticed the safe was open with petty cash strewn around in there. I don't know how it got that way, do you?"

OR

"I noticed you have been late to work every day this week, can you tell me about that?"

We discerningly acquire their side of the story with these type questions. We are garnering information which will defuse our frustration, or support an appropriate march toward a needed confrontation.

Lucy provides our organizational ER (Errand-Running). Whether it is dropping off things, picking up something else, she is usually behind the wheel. Sometimes it seems to me her errands must have involved 30 minutes with a friend for coffee or interstate commerce.

One day I was poised to jump in and accuse her of wasting time out of the office. However, restraint was king; I chose to listen first. I simply posed a non-accusatory question about her vacation, like "Hey, how'd it go out there?" before I started talking.

Lucy explained that she had to wait on items which weren't ready, how she used the time waiting to pluck additional items I desperately needed, and then traffic was wretched.

I was delighted I listened first.

> *"Those who listen to the please and cries of their people should do so patiently. Because the people want attention to what they say even more than the accomplishing for which they came."*

> *Egyptian Pharaoh Ptahhotep*

By now you should have walked discerningly through the first-half of the difficult discussions decision tree. You have searched internally by asking yourself testing questions. You have educated yourself about the conduct in question through specific non-threatening questions.

Now, you must decide what is next. You should be able to recognize if a confrontation should take place. If you believe a confrontation is in order, keep reading to learn how to deliver a message which builds team and competence . . . and won't blow up before your eyes.

Decision Branch III. Confront Honorably

Conflict is a doorway to deeper relationship . . . if it is handled well. "Well's" recipe includes many items, but its primary ingredients are, once again, honor, and its partner maturity.

First, let's address our old friend honor. Remember our goal in the process is to help our staffers and company grow. In order for this to happen, we must continue to honor our workers, with life-giving water. Infused with honor, we don't confront in a belittling matter, but realize we are all on the same team and we are responsible for our employees' growth and guidance. We must value the person we are confronting, not devalue with words and non-verbals.

Mature people are planners. They visualize the end, map their course and act accordingly. Similarly, before we arrive at our destination of team unity, we must think through how, when and where the conversation could go. Are you ready? Here we go.

Taking a look at our end is the first step. Where are we headed? Do we have our end clearly defined? Our goal may include a variety of concrete things, for example:

- Be at work on time.
- Wear clothes observing our dress code
- Balance your drawer before you leave
- Attend meetings you are asked to
- Meet your numbers

Or, they may be more subjective:

- Show more respect to your leaders
- Improve your work quality
- Get along better with those on your team

(As a reminder, we are talking about helping someone with unfavorable behavior. Try as we may, we will not be able to change someone's personality. Confrontations may reveal someone doesn't possess the skills to do a job well. However, we cannot modify who a person is.)

With your end in mind, build your case. One necessary component: you need to be very specific about the occurring offenses. From your observations, and then by being interrogative and listening well, you should have an airtight case about those offenses. If not, wait.

If you don't possess data, observances, or another one or two witnesses, you are going to have a hard time winning your case. Without support, you are in a perfect position for a bomb to go off.

For example, time clock punches revealing an offender has been late from lunch 14 times in the last 31 days puts you on solid ground. Conversely, if you have a hunch they are quitting early when you're on the road, be ready for counter-punching. The more specific you can be in your case, the less likely you are to have them turn the table on you.

When you have discussions on either end of the spectrum, there are two old rules to follow: privately rebuke, publicly praise. An old employer of mine took this adage a sensational step forward. It was his ambition to praise his team not just publicly, but specifically in front of their family members. When family members would come to the office, he would make it a point to express to them something outstanding his staff member had done.

The opposite is also true. For 95% of the time, it is important we conduct difficult discussions in private.

One surfacing concern is a private conversation with a member of the opposite sex. In these situations, try keeping the door cracked, use a glass office where others can see, or certainly include the presence of another team member. Carefully follow company rules. In today's blaming, sue-happy culture, make sure you have thought through possible consequences of a private meeting.

Time and timing are also critical components of successful conversations. Make sure you block out plenty of time for what might happen – a long discussion unfolding in a variety of directions. So, don't schedule your conversation 15 minutes before another important meeting. Even if you don't use all the time, have plenty of margin. You don't want to cut off in the middle of an important discussion, and ask to continue later in the day or after lunch.

Certainly there may be issues requiring additional thought, research and meetings. However, to not finish what can be completed in one sitting is disruptive emotionally to you and your worker.

What time of day is best? Many believe people are most open to change and new ideas when they are most alert, between 9-11 a.m. For shift workers that time would apply to their second through fourth hours on the job. For example, for a shift starting at 4 p.m., choose the hours between 5 p.m. and 7 p.m.

However, one female leader shared that she likes to have difficult conversations at the end of the day. Dayna Hayes of ConocoPhillips shares,

"In leading women, I always have my difficult reviews, hard conversations and upsetting talks starting at 4:00 or 4:30 p.m. We have enough time to talk, and if the women in my group are going to cry, it allows them to not have to spend the day at work crying and trying to hide it. They can go home and deal with the details of our discussion there. If need be, we can talk more in the morning, but by then it is mostly all worked out."

Dayna has studied her charges, is very aware of their needs, cares for their well-being and is choosing to lead them in a serving, honoring way.

Just as time is critical, so is logic.

As you look at your orchard of team members you see a variety of species. Some long to please you, others work just to be able to buy a new bass boat, and still others will stubbornly refuse to change.

To be effective, we must speak the language of the hearer.

There are several types of feedback. We'll look at three of them.

1. *Personalized Feedback:*

Most of us have lived in the personalized feedback world. Personalized feedback is subjectively driven by the one delivering it. The leader's opinion is the staffer's motivating factor. Positive statements will encourage more of the same; negative statements will dissuade it.

If a leader was given a report he didn't like and delivered personalized feedback, it would be centered on the judgments of the leader. Personalized feedback says, "I don't like the way this is written. I think it is too short and I don't like the stationery it is on." Personalized feedback is judgment by the speaker on performance.

2. *Pure Feedback:*

This more objective approach is a new concept for most managers. It is feedback that is descriptive, objective, factual, and nonjudgmental. This kind of feedback allows the receiver to decide what to do with it. It is most appropriate when the goal of a manager is to develop an independent person who can judge for themselves how they are doing—to give themselves feedback."xxxii

To apply the above example about a report being unacceptable, a leader would express pure feedback like this: "The article is only two pages long and is not on company stationery."

3. Poor Feedback:

The third type of feedback is insufficient. Poor feedback is poorly targeted, has no end in sight, can be based on presumptions and can be selfish in motivation. Feedback such as this misses the mark.

As you study the ones you lead, you will begin to understand which of the first two types of feedback serve those you lead best. Pure feedback provides personnel with more freedom and opportunity for growth. However, some personnel will only be motivated by feedback with a more personalized feel.

But it is not just our mouths. Confrontation is a discussion, not a lecture. You can learn many things from others as you listen through the confrontation. This may open a door for you to hear the roots of what is happening with your workforce.

THE NUMBER ONE RULE OF SUCCESSFUL COMMUNICATION

Communication is tricky. We all miss the mark daily. Simple things become hard. We get lost driving from basic directions. We ruin a great meal by what we put in or leave out of the food or the conversation.

As we begin our difficult conversation, we must realize the need to aim for a target. The target is the person, and we must study them as we plan for the discussion.

Whether pure or personalized feedback, we must begin to think about our specific team member – their personality, their make-up their future, their past responses.

This part of the growing process is again pruning the plant for its future fruitfulness. Farmers may choose a saw, clippers, chain-saw, or other sharp tool to trim away unhealthy growth. We too must choose the best tool for feedback, based on who our audience is.

Is the colleague clueless, insensitive, or hard-headed? Have you tried to address this issue subtly before and they just haven't heard it? You may need to make a deep, sharp cut.

An executive recently shared about a difficult conversation he had with a worker. He repeated over dinner with his wife the words he had chosen earlier in the day. "You said that to him?" she choked.

He replied that he had indeed. He had tried and tried to gain understanding from the staffer and it hadn't worked. The only way this person was going to understand was if he got hit over the head with it.

The executive went on to explain that if he continued in his current practices, he would lose his job, lose his house, and be forced to take his children out of the school associated with their workplace. His words were forceful. His target? Where it would hurt.

However, many staffers are very sensitive. For these employees, we must be sensitive to them, i.e. gently prune with an appropriate tool. Researchers tell us that about 60% of all people tend to be people-pleasing individuals who truly long to do a good job for their boss. We must keep this percentage in mind, especially if we are more motivated by task than relationship.

Staying on Track with Difficult Conversations

As we are in the planning stages of our difficult conversations, we need to be thinking about where the conversation may go. Let me share a story to illustrate.

When I graduated college, my father encouraged me to go back to school to get a graduate degree. My father was a well-educated man and wanted the same for me. He was accepted to dental school during his junior year of college, received his Doctorate in Dental Surgery, and later went back to school for a Masters in Straightening (orthodontics). It was his desire to continue his studies, but the birth of my sister and I prevented it.

I was recently looking through very old papers of his and found old tests from his master's levels classes. They were all high A's. Needless to say, he valued education.

Despite his desire for me to return to school, I shared that I didn't share the same desire. He pushed, and I pushed back. He said, "O.K., but I really think you should go." An ensuing conversation was about my summer job plans after graduation. I had a job lined up in the fall. It wasn't a career move, but was one I was looking forward to. He said, "Let me help you with a summer job." I responded with enthusiasm.

A friend of ours was the ranch manager for five huge ranches in northeastern Oklahoma. The properties were gigantic; one ranch was 45,000 acres. I served on the second smallest; a mere 23,000 acres.

The next thing I know is that it is 5:30 a.m., and I am waking up to shovel horse stalls. Every morning while it was still dark, my recently-graduated right hand was firmly attached to a shovel in a horse barn. My boss informed me the barn hadn't been shoveled out in three years and each stall had to be taken down to the bedrock. (The next semester I began working on grad-school applications).

Thankfully, lunch happened every day. And because we started so early, lunch was early. Lunch meant the end of my shoveling day and the start of a new adventure. My adventures included fence building, painting, and working cattle. Working cattle was my favorite. We dehorned, castrated, inoculated and cared for all the calves on our mere 23,000 acres.

One day we moved cattle from one pasture to another. Think *City Slickers* and you've got it. My horse, Chief, and I were behind the cattle pushing them straight ahead.

As our hips swayed on our horses slowly walking the herd, the ranch manager said to me, "You never know where these cattle may go. You've got to think ahead and be there before you get there to cut them off. They may go in a hole, the wrong way, in the woods, but beat them there and cut them off."

An opening on the right-hand side of the herd was approaching where the entire lot could go and get us all sidetracked. Chief and I listened, and soon Chief and I were up ahead of the cattle, on their right-hand side to force them toward our end goal.

As you think about where your team member may go, you must be ready to beat them there and have an answer for all kinds of responses they may have. People respond to problems with defense mechanisms. Be ready to combat their defensiveness. There are four common defense mechanisms people will employ.

Escapism is when an individual will deny or avoid dealing with a problem. At its apex you would never see this worker again after confronting them. Because of the denial factor, you must have your facts straight, solid and focused to counteract any form of denial.

Rationalization happens when someone justifies their behavior and really doesn't conceal the true motives. You might hear, as I have, that the person thought it was O.K., because another did it. Not only do you have to have your facts straight to address the specific situation, you must have your facts straight about consequences or company policy as well.

Projection involves shooting someone else's image on to another surface. For example, a movie projector shoots the images of the movie onto the screen. In this case it projection onto you. A staffer says, "I am not the one who is wrong, you are."

Displacement occurs when they blame someone else for their struggles. They may get passed over for a promotion and blame it on their ex-boss or blame it on you. They are placing the blame, incorrectly, onto another.

Before you get ready to confront, get on your horse and ride the open recesses of your confrontation. Figure out where they may take the conversation. Once there, strategize about how you will move the conversation back to the course you have directed.

LEARN FROM LINCOLN

When it came to conflict resolution, Lincoln formulated a shrewd strategy that displays why he is renowned as a leader.

When I am getting ready to reason with a man, I
spend one-third of my time thinking about myself
and what I am going to say and two-thirds about him
and what he is going to say.[xxxiii]

Abraham Lincoln

If we think our discussion is going to be confusing and full of conflict, we need to be ready to respond. Our thoughts need to be not simply on what we will say, but what will they say and how will we respond?

Use Lincoln's ratio to be ready not only for where it may go, but for bad scenarios once they try to take you there.

What is the bottom line? Success in difficult conversations requires a study of others: their thoughts, desires, and possible responses.

Decision Branch IV. Look to the Future

Pruning paint is a paint of tomorrows. Forward-looking farmers quickly apply this healing, tree salve following trimming. The paint provides protection from insects entering the affected site, it stops excessive sap-oozing and prohibits future growth out of the area addressed. Pruning paint does leave a mark on the tree revealing past pain, but also declares a farmer's interest in the tree's future.

Some farmers choose not to apply pruning paint. They simply cut and move on. Others understand the fragile nature of the wound and the need to provide protection for a healthy future.

Our honest discussions and listening ear should help us discern healthy next steps. A great team leader envisions a healthy future for all involved: his company, the team he leads and the individual. By keeping these needs central, you are in a secure position to offer:

- Coaching
- Counseling
- Discipline
- Dismissal

Some trees simply need to be staked for a period of time. They will grow straight. They will grow well, and they will produce fruit with tension being provided for them. Some of your employees may fit this description. Do they simply need *coaching*? If you have delivered honoring correction and determined the person means well, and wants to change behavior, you have gained an ally. Now, you can strengthen the bond by gracefully coaching them through change.

For example, if your worker has not executed due to fear, coach them through it. For example, you could say, "Jim, I want you to sit in with me during my next conversation as I offer the warranty to our customer. You can learn the process. Then I'll sit in with you as you offer it to another customer."

Movement from confrontation to future, should focus on improvement. One helpful key in leadership is the ageless adage, "progress not perfection".

An outside party may also be enlisted to coach. Either way, the worker understands you are on their team. They may have made mistakes, but you are leading them to a solution. This type of leadership bonds.

Counseling

Does your team member long to do the right thing, but needs professional help to pull it off? A young man approached me with issues beyond my understanding – deeply rooted addiction issues.

At times, my lay counseling seemed helpful. So, I would settle in, listening actively and encourage him in his personal struggles. Yet, ultimately traction was lost, and we were back to the same plaguing problems.

He wisely talked to another who challenged him to seek professional help. While I was listening well and doing my best, I was not solving the issue. A professional counselor could, and did.

The man is now flourishing; he needed more help than I could provide. Professional counseling was the right play.

Discipline

A wise person will listen to a rebuke[xxxiv]. If they understand the consequences of their choices, your correction may have easily changed their behavior. Most corporations have a company policy of discipline to follow. If you are running a small corporation, you can establish fair principles. However, think through consequences. Don't rashly announce consequences for behavior which cannot be enforced. You will either discipline or dismiss people needlessly, or lose respect as a leader.

Coaching and counseling provide opportunities for you to easily show staff you are honoring them, serving them, and providing a healthy environment for them to succeed.

Discipline, on the other hand, may be more difficult for your staffers to see as employee care. However, difficult times in a relationship -- if they are handled well -- are truly the path to unity. As the leader of the organization, it is up to you to pursue the team member for relational rebuilding. They may run from you, be afraid of you, and not want a relationship with you. As the person in the position of authority, you must be the pursuer. Through your follow-up actions, display to your worker you are truly interested in them, their future and the company.

Dismissal

In 2005, huanglongbing, also known as "citrus greening", was discovered in orange groves in Florida. Prices on a box of oranges from 2004 to 2012 had increased 175% because of the devastating nature it had on the groves.[xxxv] The only alternative was to remove infected trees before they infected the rest. Similarly, that might be what is best for your team.

One thing is certain. Any type of feedback no matter how well-planned, organized, and perfectly-executed does not guarantee results. "The problem with communication is the illusion that it has been accomplished," said George Bernard Shaw.

Your worker may not have a teachable heart or be willing to grow. Their apathy may be revealed immediately, or all the more as you talk with them.

So what do you do if one you lead doesn't listen? First, follow your corporate policy. It will save you and your team from potential lawsuits and other problems. Dismissal can be a blessing to your team and to the one dismissed.

A colleague of mine has dismissed dozens. He shares it is not unusual to later be thanked for moving them forward in their career. Often those staffers know they are in the wrong position, but a career change is a too difficult move to make. When he has made it for them, they later share their gratitude.

We must not lose sight of our central focal point of success—to look out for the best for the company and the employees. With those goals in mind, dismissal may fit best.

My story is very similar. I was not let go for bad conduct, I just was not a good fit.

The first part of my professional career was fundraising. My career trajectory seemed to have been launched. In 2002, my second daughter was two months old, my wife and I had owned our first home first home together for 1 month, and we were a growing, happy family. Yet, I was struggling at work with vision, passion and "fit".

Then I was let go.

It may have been one of the best things ever for me vocationally.

I then spent many hours soul-searching. Speaking and teaching were my natural skills. I'd always wanted to do those things; although, fundraising was what I knew, where my experience lived. I dreaded the work. I interviewed for a few positions to raise money. A pit gripped my stomach each time.

Then one day a friend asked if I could train a mid-sized local organization. "Of course I could," I responded enthusiastically. I had zero experience, but plenty of passion. After hours and hours of preparation, the appointed day came. I was nervously green and inexperienced, but prepared. After my several hour delivery, my hosts loved it and so did I!

I am grateful for the opportunity given to look elsewhere for employment. Dismissal has allowed me to use God-given skills and enjoy the ease of using them. In my old position, I was swimming upstream, while now, I feel like I am swimming with flippers on.

Secrets of Sequoias

No tree proclaims strength, stability and majesty like the Sequoias. These massive beasts can grow as high as a 38 story building. These trees can become up to 26 feet in diameter.

Stephen Stillett studies sequoias, also known as redwoods. One of his favorites is known as The President. The President, named after Warren Harding, is 93 feet in circumference and with 45,000 cubic feet of trunk volume and another 9,000 cubic feet in its branches. Sliced into one-foot by one-foot cubes, it would cover a football field.[xxxvi]

Stillett has been studying their leaves in relationship to the climate. The President has over 2 BILLION leaves. Not only does it impact the health of those species growing close to it, Stillett and his team are working on equations to uncover how large a shadow these trees cast in relationship to the absorption of planet-warming carbon dioxide.

When fire comes, it only irritates them. Their bark is too thick. They laugh at high winds and enjoy the breeze through their leaves.

Yet, despite the health of their conditions – great soil, their tops reaching out for even more sunshine, that is not what makes them so strong.

They are the only species on the planet that intermingles itself at the roots. They are bound for life with their peers; they support each other through high winds, fire and lightning strikes through depth of unity unseen.

As you have built your team with sincere care and service, honor, servant leadership, daily care and honest, graceful correction, you can stand confidently. You have created allies, fellow sequoias who will be burying their roots when difficult times come. They too will be intermingled with you as your company stands above the skyline of your city firmly tied together and bearing fruit for your community and perhaps the world.

ABOUT THE AUTHOR

Great Communication has been a passion for Chris Zervas since he was first asked to speak in front his local Rotary Club at the age of 17.

Army National Guard Bureau, US Bank, and ConocoPhillips are among the organizations Chris has helped to improve communication processes and results. His writings have appeared in periodicals and websites such as Entrepreneur.com.

In 1990 Chris received his Master's Degree in Communication from Wheaton College. He then worked for a decade in the non-profit arena with communication gurus such as Joe White and Gary Smalley.

Two college faculties have employed Chris' expertise in the areas of speech and business communication. In 2005, Chris began to specialize in leading corporate employees, improving their presentation and interpersonal communication skills, which impacts their bottom line.

Chris lives with his wife and children in Oklahoma.

i http://www.usna.usda.gov/

ii Heskett, James L., Jones, Thomas O., Loveman, Gary W., Sasser, W. Earl, and Schelsinger, Leonard A. "Putting the Service Profit Chain to Work", Harvard Business Review, (March–April 1994) 164-174.

iii ibid

iv See From Engagement to Work Passion © 2009 Ken Blanchard Company.

v www.tompeters.com/slides/uploaded/060908_3H-6H.ppt

vi Holy Bible. Pr. 28:23 New Living Translation (NLT) copyright© 1996, 2004, 2007 by Tyndale House Foundation.

vii http://www.merriam-webster.com/dictionary/honor

viii Smith, Jean Edward. Grant. New York: Simon & Schuster, 2001. Print.

ix http://lincolninstitute.wordpress.com/2011/05/31/lincoln-as-a-servant-leader/

x Hunter

xi Hunter

xii Rose, Lacey (November 18, 2005). "The Single Greatest Athletic Achievement". Forbes.com.

xiii NLT John 15:13.

xivhttp://lincolninstitute.wordpress.com/2011/05/31/lincoln-as-a-servant-leader/

xv Uldrich, Jack. Soldier, Statesman, Peacemaker: Leadership Lessons from George C. Marshall. New York: AMACOM, 2005.

xvi Adapted from Ken Blanchard companies (November 2008), "Delivering Well Crafted, Targeted Feedback", Ignite

xvii Ibid

xvii http://lincolninstitute.wordpress.com/2011/05/31/lincoln-as-a-servant-leader/

xviii Blanchard, Kenneth H., and Spencer Johnson. The One Minute Manager. New York: Morrow, 1982. Print

xixxix Rath, T., & Clifton, D. O. (2004). How full is your bucket? Positive strategies for work and life. New York: Gallup Press.

xx Adapted from Josh McDowell.

xxi Ibid

xxii Ibid

xxiii Losada, M. "The Complex Dynamics of High Performance Teams." Mathematical and Computer Modelling 30.9-10 (1999): 179-92. Print.

xxiv Frederickson, B. "Positive Emotions and Upward Spirals in Organizations." Presented at the Gallup World Conference, Omaha, Ne (2003).

xxv Mary Ellen Guffey, Essentials of Business Communication, 6e, Ch. 11.

xxvi Blanchard, and Johnson. The One Minute Manager.

xxvii NLT Tyndale House Foundation. Pr. 28:23.

xxviii The Holy Bible, New International Version (NIV). James 1:9 Grand Rapids: Zondervan House, 1984. Print.

xxix Ibid James 4:1

xxx Blanchard, Ignite.

xxxi Corporate Resource Council white paper, 2002.

xxxii Blanchard, Ignite.

xxxiiihttp://www.brainyquote.com/quotes/quotes/a/abrahamlin 164051.html

xxxiv NIV Pr. 15:31

xxxv http://www.huffingtonpost.com/2013/08/30/citrus-greening_n_3780984.html

xxxvi http://www.huffingtonpost.com/2012/12/01/the-president-giant-sequoia_n_2224855.html

Made in the USA
San Bernardino, CA
26 May 2015